What Love Is

by

Kerry Darbishire

The moment was all;

the moment was enough.

Virginnia Woolf

First published 2026 by The Hedgehog Poetry Press,
5 Coppack House, Churchill Avenue, Clevedon. BS21 6QW
www.hedgehogpress.co.uk
Copyright © Kerry Darbishire 2026
The right of Kerry Darbishire to be identified as the author of this work has been asserted in accordance with the Copyright, Designs and Patents Act 1988. All rights reserved. No part of this publication may be reproduced, stored in or introduced into a retrieval system, or transmitted in any form, or by any means (electronic, mechanical, photocopying, recording or otherwise) without prior written permissions of the publisher. Any person who does any unauthorised act in relation to this publication may be liable for criminal prosecution and civil claims for damages.
ISBN: 978-1-916830-58-5

for Steve

and all the years

of your love

Contents

Love 7
You Ask Me Why I Stay 8
For the love of a fellside 9
Wallers 10
Moss 11
If You are Listening.. 12
Miss Aileen's Snowdrops... 13
Oak Tree.. 14
That this would last.. 15
How Can I Tell You... 16
From Questel to Plouézec 17
Finding my way back along Compston Road 18
I Dream of Him 19
The Bridesmaid.. 20
From A Balcony 21
Olive Grove 22
Catching November Light.. 23
November 5th 24
What Love Is.. 25
Christmas Landscape... 26

Bust of Delius 27
In the wooden house 28
Heirlooms 29
What matters now 30
Roll Top 31
Power Cut 32
My body is a house in winter 33
To the One I love 34
Quilt 35
Yorkshire Spreads like Mill Cloth 36
Last Letter from Caitlin to Dylan 37
Your Letter – Ghazal 38
Wolf at my Window 39
To fill the space 40
In the garden where we sit together 41
A Place for Winter 42
Take me with you 43
Pine needles on the windowsill 44
ACKNOWLEDGEMENTS 46

LOVE

There was a time I couldn't say your name.
Something with the vowel sound, the mix
of being born in the south, raised in the north –
never hearing my mother say *I love you* to my father.
    My mouth refused to find the right shape.

Stay with me. There was a time I was sunlight
on moving water and I'd say: I like, quite like, really like,
head-over-heels, mad about, until one evening you appeared
dressed in a stunning kiss – the shock
    of a racing heart, glamour devouring every cell

of my body, yet saying your name out loud was mist
clearing from a lake, no, slower. Only you
could have shown me sycamore buds
swelling one by one like stars in a spring sky,
    shown me autumn leaves falling

sometimes rushed by the wind but always with grace leaf by leaf
smothering the ground in glorious yellows,
reds, browns. Only you could have shown me
how to say without thinking, I love
    I love you.

YOU ASK ME WHY I STAY

after Ocean Vuong

To remember our first winter together.

For wild geese returning north and south in waves of song.

To watch morning sun pour itself down the fell like honey on bread.

To hear you strike a match in the blackened hearth.

For the first two notes of a cuckoo in May.

For a glass of fell water. Moon-soaked fields. Your breath upon the frosty air.

To know the next thing.

To see three pheasants roosting in the pine tree outside my window.

For your touch lovely as a ripe apple I didn't eat straight away.

To watch a goldcrest caper on stems of clematis.

Because my children will always want to ask me something.

To watch your gift of bluebells spread like a wide fallen sky.

For the air through my bedroom window carrying night sound.

For rain in all her moods.

For your river of words always knowing which way to flow.

To say the things I haven't learned yet.

FOR THE LOVE OF A FELLSIDE

after *The Lost Garden of Loughrigg*
- Penn Allen

Imagine a spring day drawing out possibilities
the newness of life, sisters in long skirts digging
tangled ground, breaking bones and loam wild
with bracken and rock on this south facing slope.

Then, the building of an enclosure to protect plants
from deer and sheep. Long ago this affair
before my mother walked me up a sweeping track
to be wrapped in scented blooms nurtured from seedlings -

cuttings - discoveries posted from wildest China:
Primula Purdomii for stars, *Gentian* for sky,
Viburnum for fragrance - treasures arriving each week
in packages - perennials for sun, for shade to be planted

in harmony. A garden with a view to the Langdale Pikes
and air once breathed never left your lungs,
and cool damp mist rising from the River Brathay
in mornings reluctant to let go the night. All this

what it was to be here, the guardians waking each day
to seven acres of crag knowing your hands and heart
belong to this patch of earth.

WALLERS

Beyond meadowsweet and eglantine
under a map of stars – the milky way – the whites
of eyes on screes, they bivvied month after month
building the *ring garth* – the divide between wild

and cultivated land. Men and boys hefted to the fell,
heaving beck boulders, heartings, throughs and cams
to keep flocks out and in. Their backs bent as bracken,
against the yowl of the northerly that gathered in

the first snows. Fingers thistle-sharp, stubborn as ice,
on they laboured through gale and rain, following rise
and fall, cobble and slip through thicket and dyke,
each burrow and lair in the Helm-wind air until

skylarks broke silence and summer-green slopes
sprang wick with gorse and foxgloves and the hollow-stem
claim of owls and vixen-hunger ran fast as becks
through their veins.

MOSS

> Jophiel Wiis (Astrophysicist in Copenhagen) uses the phrase,
> *romantic idea*, to think that moss could survive on Mars.

Like a hatchling bound in lush green names:
Juniper, White Heart, Grandfather's Beard,
Sphagnum and Spiral, I lay in woven scent
of pepper, cucumber, oysters, dreaming

of a life on Mars. In a bed of rootless green
that led me back over millions of years – a journey
through rise and fall of winters, wounded summers
to the taste of rain, spores spinning

like fireworks through night air, I found a symbiosis
with men and women who sweep leaves from its surface,
who worship temples of tiny kingdoms in Yakusugi
where Giant Cedars grow sustained by messages

of water from moss to roots. I found camouflage
where Golden Plovers raise chicks nested in the safety
of feathery fingers taking and giving the thing we need most –
spreading and spreading like mist on a river.

I found to die many times and return to possess rock, woods
and pasture is the alchemy of existence, deep worlds
multiplying from a single bird-thin stem.

IF YOU ARE LISTENING

after Jen Hadfield – for Krissy

Let me have this day, the orchard, rhubarb
pink as piglets gambling in muddy earth,
mist in damson trees setting Spring.

Let me have snowdrops thick as party frills,
the ghyll still mourning lack of rain,
air sweet with gorse from the fell,

a woodpecker morse-coding sycamores
the shiny coat of newborn lambs, echo of geese
forewarning strangers at the gate.

Let me have a winter sky, each star a friend
I've known and loved, a summer's afternoon
my dog sprawled sleeping by the porch

at the end of the day
so I may dream my life again.

MISS AILEEN'S SNOWDROPS

Spring begins to blot out bare umber earth
  in a chatter of nodding heads that gather and race
    in a honey scent of lengthening days
      towards the river's edge.

For every child she taught, snowdrops drift the slope
  of her garden, around rocks and brash carrying
    good news from her neat beds of azaleas,
      primrose and aconites.

Her bent figure, gloved fingers working leafy borders,
  planting each bulb eager to see us spill
    like morning milk, faster than winter sunlight
      into the world. I want to tell her now

how she made the difference – her voice warm as tea
  when she said, *well done*, reading our seedling pages
    as if she'd made a discovery, heeling in belief, releasing us
      to shine like her pearl earrings she couldn't unfasten.

OAK TREE

The heel and sink of a shovel into soil that spring
    to plant a cracked seed I held in one hand

like a wren's egg. A husk eager to split
    and grow in the soak of leaves –

composted stories buried beneath my feet.
    In darkness I said your name over –

starting with O and ending with a season
    of sudden snow charming northern air.

How easily you balance sun and moons now
    on your bare shoulders, how you load July air

with sweetness and shade. How bark grows rough
    with age. Guardian of forget-me-nots, windflowers

you bring the spring of a nesting song-thrush, the chime
    of children playing long after bedtime.

THAT THIS WOULD LAST

There was only the steady gaze of Loughrigg
over Benson's hayfield waist high
when we lay in the safetynet of summer
stretched like owl's wings over the muddy edge
    of the river.

There were only sticks, string and bent pins
cast for trout and perch twisting between
old moorings – rotten posts and slimy stones
in the silence of Sunday evenings.
   There was only the changing light

cool cloak of dusk stowed with secrets of pine,
wings brushing our skin, mists of insects
wrestling the surface, gaping mouths snatching
one then another down into the deepest bed
    leaving only a sway of stars.

HOW CAN I TELL YOU

    i.m. Caroline Gilfillan

Last month they read your poems
   traced your journey   savoured your words
     slipped into places they'd never been –

lines took flight   from pages you sent like parcels
   of Indian spices. Verses you'd selected like the handling
    of a wounded bird. While storms hit England

and leaves fell from Summer to Autumn   you
   still flared yellow   copper and red – the way
    maples can light a coastline. You'd planned ahead

your notebooks not quite full. Yesterday your path was clear
   until mist drove you off course. Leaving was not
    your choice. We were swans travelling as far as we could go

through sky and snow   thermals ruffling
  our feathers   high on finest air.
   Today was a sharp breath –

you've been listed in a competition.
  How can I tell you the good news
   through all this snow?

FROM QUESTEL TO PLOUÉZEC

after *Déjeuner du matin* - Jacques Prévert

She rode her bike –
a stranger
for too long
   she kept faith
with the morning
pedalled slowly
along roads
steady as canals
rows of cauliflowers
beginning to touch
the green of each other
   she kept faith
with the distance
smiled and sang
make you feel my love
smooth as pebbles
on Pors Pin beach
ripe as the apples
falling in gardens
   she kept faith
with the company
of birds and sun
and the village
where a man at a table
   kept faith with pastis
she watched smoke
chug from his lips
he watched the to and fro
at *Lesenfantsdubulanger*
he didn't speak
or look at her
she rode her bike
she cried

FINDING MY WAY BACK ALONG COMPSTON ROAD

to the first climbing shop that promised rope
and Carabiner safety on Gimmer Crag, Clayton's
marble slab of warm livers and hearts running red
as rivers, Mrs Hewitt's knick-knack parlour
sparkling with faux moonstone earrings that hung
like lanterns from our Saturday-soft ears, the trust
in Tinny Martin's ironmongery where anything
was possible between shelves of paper serviettes,
radiator paint and gossip beneath the top-shelf mags'
where best mates whispered dreading the school bell
that dragged us back into the arena of verbs and rift valleys
on a Friday afternoon dreaming of the weekend
that promised lacquered hair, and cool, in heels parading
the wet-gummed street to the cinema – a dozen steps up
into Doris Day's log cabin, John Wayne's saloon bar,
Bambi, Lorna Doone – music that kept us singing for days,
then later, much later, the back row kissing Ken
the weekend biker from Wigan who tried to go too far, but
with the smell of chips and leather on our lips, we promised
to keep in touch held in the glow of the Sports Club
where old Henry staggered and swore like a plundered ship
but always someone to save him from drowning.

I DREAM OF HIM

amongst lime-crinkled walls
greased boskins smooth as milk,
leaning into pillowed udders
easing out the summer's day
   singing *Blue Moon.*

I carry his tune across the yard
to a bale-barricaded lane
in and out of the sun
where an upturned roof-ridge
   works field water into Barkin Beck,

rills heather, peat and marigolds to a deep well
long lost in the lean and crack of willows.
Where we first met
driving our breathy flocks to Kendal market
   his eyes bright as a new moon and mine

spring-shy and barely a word
all the way there.
Meadow-rolled tyres now sunk in verdigris
and rows of logs, tell me winter will soon
   be carried to the hearth.

I remember the heat in his hands
on mornings when frost
ferned the bedroom window
we lay folded, still
   and unafraid.

THE BRIDESMAID

Oil on panel by John Everett Millais, 1851

Love was but a seedling planted in Tennyson –
a poem I found wrapped around a block
of butter. I was twenty-two, making hats
for Mrs Tozer, dreaming of a marriage
    to someone like Millais.

It was the spring of times, my dawn-grey eyes
looking towards a new day, my mouth
soft as a fledgling song-thrush ready to receive.
He asked me to hold a ring and piece
    of cake as it was believed:

> *that if a piece of wedding cake was passed*
> *through a ring nine times, a bridesmaid*
> *would see a vision of her true love.*

In the slow hours of that studio
my waist-length hair brushed and burning
like an autumn hillside beneath a night sky,
he fastened an orange-blossom brooch to my silk-
    embroidered yellow dress, his scent so close.

FROM A BALCONY

after Marie Spartali Stillman

no fuss   no jewellery   skin   studio-pale
my olive-green eyes looking indirectly at you   yes

as if I have something to hide
did I tell you   *I find portraits very nervous work*

I'll catch the silence of a moment to myself
the immobility of the Mediterranean at midday

my dress will be   a palette of dried blood
night secrets caught in folds of silk   highlights to echo

those bright Aegean mornings I remember   but
instead of a knife   like Lady Macbeth

I'll hold a fan   the haunting blue sea   below   yes
the view

OLIVE GROVE – Saint-Rémy-de-Provence

after Olive Trees – Vincent Van Gogh

I came here to dance amongst violet shadows
brave the Mistral surging Prussian-blue hills

impasto scraping this land like hail.
I came here not to see almond blossom fall

or the birth of a spring sky, but to smell the sand-
dry earth, to see how fruit clusters in the dark heat

of Provence caught in the turmoil of olive trees,
their feet trapped unable to lift towards the moon-eyed

cloud – the yellow and pink of it looming over the backs
of the Chaîne des Alpilles like a father's fury.

He could have gone anywhere after Paris, but came here
where he could work without knowing it.

I would rather die of passion than boredom. But
no fruit falls. It should have been *divine* –

his garden of Gethsemane, this storm churning
waiting to break.

CATCHING NOVEMBER LIGHT

Start with a warm ground
    move quickly

clouds loom like bears
    crossing the valley   shadows grow long as pine trees

holding on to those last rays   slip titanium white
    over impasto rocks to reach the river   stars splash

fast-flowing water   consider burnt umber
    deep beneath the surface   this is where in summer

leeches hide in moss-darkness and perch slide the cold silty
    canvas bed   a breeze stipples ash and oak revealing

touches of orange and lemon-yellow   work faster
    notice the glimmer between the palette of greens

and raw sienna leaves   reflecting the story of warmer days
    an owl sits at the top of a sycamore watching

for movement   listening for the brush of indigo
    and ultramarine   accents of snow

NOVEMBER 5TH

Today we made our pledge,
    with a pin became blood sisters.

Today we missed the school bus,
    ran three miles home between stars.

Today I sat in a London office typing sounds
    of the mountains I'd left behind.

Today I fell in love in a garden
    of fallen apples and sulphur mist

sky wrapped the fells
    in thin tissue, mizzle dripped

from bare trees onto my anorak
    and slid down my neck like a first kiss.

Today the valley closed like a frozen window,
    numb as an emptied house.

Today wore a scarf of leaves
    catherine wheels spun and I thought of you.

Today I gathered all the things I couldn't say
    but need to tell you now.

WHAT LOVE IS

To know your palette
is not just a marriage of colour

To see how you brush raw umber
like deep earth over a white field

To smell turpentine on your shirt
your arms around me

warmth on my neck
remembering who we were

CHRISTMAS LANDSCAPE

Wrapped in kitchen warmth
I stride out taking it with me
over fields under hedges,
all pigment erased, burnt umber
buried beneath a palette of tinsel-white.
Only the flame of a robin in a hawthorn
singing like a distant bell
catches the still air.

Across the valley sheep huddle
around bales of last summer, breath
rising like ancient signals: clover, vetch,
yellow rattle. I crunch on.
You show me how a winter sky glows
raw sienna against drifts, the name
of each tone: Paynes grey, indigo, flake white,
and how pines and holly by the river folded in ice

is worked with a palette knife.
You lay out the deep language of rabbit, fox
and hare dashed across a hungry canvas,
signatures stamped in flourishes of twos
and threes. By Judy's gate
I press an apple into Joey's soft muzzle
then double back, your hand in mine
brushed with snow.

BUST OF DELIUS

He was always going somewhere - Eric Fenby

He stares out as if about to stand and walk
across a summer lawn for a clearer pitch
of water, finch, cuckoo - drawn to tones
of nature like a butterfly to nectar.

His blind gaze feeling for new colours,
placing, for the first time, flutes and strings
in a particular soundscape, a particular morning
when water flowed down his spine like love.

I touch his half-lidded eyes, thumbed plaster-
of-Paris - grey-greased with age, in search for more
than his *song of the high hills,* to quarry translations
of Florida, Paris, mountains, silence of a lost child.

IN THE WOODEN HOUSE

after Margaret Atwood

dismantled board by board and burned, I'm listening to rain
on the felt roof and owls in the pines on the edge of the garden
no longer mine.

Morning light limps through large windows, last night's ashtrays
still full. My mother can't find her bedroom, has lost her dogs
and the summer curtains don't fit.

She cannot shut herself away from dreams of walking.
Her clothes hang like garden borders, dressing table
all lavender and powder. I make her strong black coffee

the way she likes it. Where is her favourite painting
of Moonlight on Loughrigg Tarn? A pale empty square
hangs in the hall. The mirror too is foxed, reflecting

a moon-faced nine year old, cutting hair with kitchen scissors
in a corridor of damp honeysuckle wallpaper and the sound
of the river washing me back to the smell of fresh paint,

Sunday wireless, my brother and sister laughing
because I don't understand the word, *concerto.*
In the house with its Rachmaninov-soaked tongue

and groove walls, the Sheila Maid dripping school uniforms
and stained sheets. I watch morning spread like fell-mist
through the kitchen no longer here,

Mum is singing *Fly Me to the Moon,* I'm picking up marbles
from the red linoleum floor, waiting for the arrival
of her mother, long-gone.

HEIRLOOMS

Stone murmurs darkness, wild scent
of meadows sweated through cart-wide
doors on August evenings where Maybugs
lashed sultry air between glinting scythes, rakes
    and pitchforks hanging from riddled rafters.

On a fellside where seasons fly like owls hunting
snow light, stripped by the Helm wind each March
no one walks by, talks to the dead: a father's
tobacco-drenched desk, a mother's blue and white
    crockery mothed in dust, sheet music

folded and foxed like the plague, and souls lingering
still afraid of the Spanish flu, two wars, tables bloomed
in conversation – all-nighters on Shelley, Delius, Tolstoy,
someone in the corner too drunk to stand and falling
    like hatchlings from slapdash nests, between cabriole legs

and splat-backs crumbling in winters, wanting release
from the burden of, *nobody wants brown furniture*, begging,
let us go, give us away, burn us while we still have some dignity.
But it's never the right time, the right weather, it's always
    next summer, always next summer.

WHAT MATTERS NOW

is the first day of no snow
and the first snowdrops
pressing through raw earth
    into a vase of brightness

into a longer day
unexpectedly received like a blessing
beginning to stretch   and glisten
like the fur on my dog's back
    the kindness

of sun sinking into her spine
through skin   muscle
her flock-gathering blood
the joy of her tail spinning
    like spent leaves in a sudden breeze.

She's running   and running
her wintered paws
over wet turf   nose to trail
of pheasant   fox
    and hare.

She stops.
Raises her front paw mid-air
and in this moment
    her wild beating heart.

ROLL TOP

Rescued for a tenner from a scrap yard
rusty, still as a ewe caught in a drift of snow
waiting to be crushed, a body of iron
asking to be bought back to life, regain
      the same heat as the height of summer.

Once bathing was at the heart of civilisation
in ancient Pakistan, the hygienic thing to do
in the palace of Knossos, Crete, when tin
and iron replaced water-tight bitumen-lined bricks
      in rooms decorated with frescoes.

We fell in love many times with baths
corroding against hedges, abandoned by gates,
claw and ball feet standing their ground,
overflowing with spring water, dreaming
      their great weight lugged up a narrow staircase

to the luxury of inside plumbing, home late
from hedging February lanes, soaking our bones
in cast-iron-heat – a roll-top full
and steaming in a lime-washed room
      with a view to the meadow.

POWER CUT

We'd forgotten the smell of tallow,
    flicker of candles, dancing chairs
on lime-washed walls, sound of hail
    shifting to snow against the window.

We'd forgotten the warmth of logs
    the grate – aglow with conversation
on the coldest night of the year. Outside
    the silence of stars and moon

over fields of snow sending us
    all the light we needed.

MY BODY IS A HOUSE IN WINTER

Hope is a thing with feathers – Emily Dickinson

latched in frost   veins   rivers
stilled   and   slow
as dying blood   skin
pale as pale as skin can be   desire
snowbound and words confined
to lakes that cannot breathe
                                    If I could fly
through corridors   scented rooms
a favourite painting to lift me to a house
where light and bowls we cherished   blossomed
on a table laid for spring
                                    summer will
find me in a harebell sky   drifts of lightest rain
birds nesting without fear
sea-lapped curlews   singing
from new-moon beaks
                                    and summer
will   beat these wings along landings   bright
and scented as a Vita Sackville-West garden
where the first roses   hollyhocks   peonies
will be opening their hearts
by a wooden seat in a yard
nodding with bees

TO THE ONE I LOVE

I have saved this afternoon for you
- T.S. Eliot

when all was at its height
softness slipped our fingers:

rosa rubrifolia, sweet william,
buddleia, amulets of butterflies
giddying the afternoon.

We went about being in the garden
whilst in a garden

of bright wings, mint tea
and plans unfolding new
as snow falling upon a winter lawn

summer hours pouring through us
smooth as citrine wax

burning our room of flowers

QUILT

Patching is an ancient thing to do in the slowing months.
Cotton shirts he'd bought from a market in Italy- stalls
piled high, three for two, worn at weddings and funerals.
Gingham ripped climbing over Joss's fence, Flannelette
muck-smeared from the hen coop, grass stains from rolling
Pasche eggs down Hoad Hill. Pinafore dresses hand-sewn
to keep her children smart and warm, gather in spills
and arguments, kisses and birthdays. Lighter days briefly
forgotten begin to appear like crystals in a winter sky.
Running her fingers over the pathways of Dobby, Winceyette,
Seersucker - the taste of Persian words, *shir o shedar - mild and sugar*,
she's making sense of textures shifting like the uncertainty
of rivers where they swam and reeled in perch. A marriage
all over again, eager to make home a drift of roses, borders
of lavender, new moons. A murmuration of starlings appliquéd
tone on tone to intakes, spread up the fell to velvet clouds basting
the horizon. She knows a square inch of Liberty fabric can draw
the eye to hedges and lanes in the way southbound geese cry.
She threads an easterly to the valley where sun streamed
through windows early and blazed a William Morris orchard
in the golden hour before stoats and blackbirds hunkered in dusk.
Making a land from Irish linen tablecloths, sleeves and scarves
she'd washed and ironed a thousand times, she cuts, layers
and stitches to keep her bones from aching as the nights draw in.

YORKSHIRE SPREADS LIKE MILL CLOTH

From Leeds to Preston the train weaves
    villages and towns under bridges,
past thickets of birch, embankments
    littered with broken basins and toilets, prams
and chairs discarded like hanks of wool.
    We wind over sodden fields pounded
by cattle to fodder, through Halifax, Hebden Bridge,
    Sowerby Bridge with platforms of girls
their hair thick and strong as ponies manes,
    breath wefting air.
Terraced houses thread a tangle of hills,
    empty mills perch between trees bare -
leaves rusting the ground, valleys and rivers grey
    as flocks passing through old darkness
        that brushes your skin.
In the warmth of this carriage I'm reading
    Laurie Lee - folk working village to village
when birds and stars seemed closer and everything
    depended on the time of year.
And on we glide hopeful as shuttles that once
    belonged to Alfred Brown, Joshua Ellis,
Abraham Moon. November allotments slip by
    silent as factory looms, lip-reading weavers,
strings of onions hanging in sheds,
    broad beans drying, old rollers, heddles,
beams - things that might come in.

LAST LETTER FROM CAITLIN TO DYLAN

Rome - overlooking the Tiber, 1976

Oh, how I miss our chats my love, soft and green
   as the valley, you dishevelled and interesting
      downing liquor, drowning fast in the search for words
and me trying to keep up with shots of whisky.
   I was lost to know what to do when I found you
      barely past youth, not raging but lying gentle
in an oxygen tent, already gone. I almost offered you
   a drag on my rollup wanting to ask, *was it my dress -*
   all flowers and blowing in the salt wind? when we never
stopped talking, then fell into bed together as if we had always
   known each other. Do you remember
      sitting in your offstage slippers eating a dish of titbits:
pickled onions, cockles, sardines? Poverty didn't
   squeeze through the window like moonlight, it was already here.
      Yes, you made your money but we paid dearly.
America ate you up.
   I'm thinking clearly now for the first time in my life -
      and loving this Latin way of living even though wine and men
are out of reach.
   I don't regret sharing you with the world, I loved and wanted
      to kill you in equal measure. How marvellous we were,
me wandering the estuary, you pondering long afternoons
   on a single line.

   This is how I'll remember you,

      Your Caitlin xxxxx

YOUR LETTER – GHAZAL

Your letter was a swallow returned   I found
a long-awaited bird   I found

the sound of sea and sand   the loop
of darkness I unfurled   I found

each *s* a smile   each line a hug
the meaning of each letter's curve   I found

love roosted on each row and stitch
winged through the plain and purl   I found

your message was the warmth I wore
a jumper patching winter's hurt   I found

your *o* and *r* the missing years
summered in your letter's words

WOLF AT MY WINDOW

Your hands soft as rain on a summer's day
    in a field of seedlings   your breath on my shoulder
you gift me back what the years scythe away
    the hunger   the famine as we grow older.

In a field of seedlings   your breath on my shoulder
    I still dream of sex when the long nights set in
the hunger   the famine as we grow older
    your hands warm as fur on my creasing skin.

I still dream of sex when the long nights set in
    love howls outside like a wolf at my window
your hands warm as fur on my creasing skin
    I wait for you as each autumn gets colder.

Love howls outside like a wolf at my window
    your hands soft as rain on a summer's day
so often I think of the fire that still smoulders
    you gift me back what the years scythe away.

TO FILL THE SPACE

I leave the radio on in the kitchen, pretend
he's still here mixing cadmium yellow into umber
to lay sun into a forest, his arm aching,

brushing in a mass of blue sky above thousands
of leaves that grew and fell into the emptiness
of a terrible year.

I leave the radio on to fill the space
he called *my studio*, it warms the air, somehow
brings life to his dry palette, the oversized table,

empty chairs. I leave the radio on to hear
Jeremy Vine, fears of the helpless who rely
on the kindness of others working

long shifts night after night to save someone else.

IN THE GARDEN WHERE WE SIT TOGETHER

I wait for news   holding my breath.
        Snowdrops nod catching a breeze.
I'm told he's through the worst and awake.

Above me wild geese are heading north
        in splintered lines   through shifting clouds.
I think of the nurses   connecting tubes   monitoring

repeated patterns in   green   yellow   blue.
        When I ring   he tells me broken things
I remind myself it's the anaesthetic   the anaesthetic

I won't ask him how or where he is
        he's blown off-course.   There are strangers
in the ward   at three in the morning

crying fear   roars of thunder
        dread of wind   men shouting
like sticks snapping from branches.

I remember my mother   abstractions
        falling from her lips   her eyes buried too far
below the surface.   She never knew there was a last day.

I tell him there's a spring lawn waiting   morning stars
        gliding through celandines
blackbirds calling the air.

A PLACE FOR WINTER

With winged heart   the rush of a blackbird's song
the graze of love   she is herself   at last   unafraid

of dreams that fall in the shelter of dawn   the half light
of late November. She questions the distance   motherhood

mistakes she's made   her father gone at her age.
She thinks of swallows   Morocco in their feathers

salt coursing their lungs   swooping into the byre   then
the emptiness of telephone wires as fog sets in.

She remembers Haw Lonning   honeysuckle
dripping from wild arms   Autumn shadows worn long

like scarves wrapping woods and tarns   two kestrels
circling the barn   and what it was to stand in the damp pantry

listening to wise women   storing apples   how to salt a pig
make soup from leftovers.

Outside   an oak tree casts another year in a shatter
of old gold. A wasp at the window is finding a place

the sting of summer looping her wings.

TAKE ME WITH YOU

I'm sure he says   as I close the door
    and step out into the field

glistening turf   distant fells the palest sapphire blue
    cut by a single pall of wood smoke

rising above glints of beck like a snagged scarf.
    And there   John's farm folded into his uncle's land

where once oats were harvested   I stand
    thinking   *how long have we been here?*

Crows echo serious messages from tree
    to each bare tree   a pheasant sets up

like burnt paper from winter ashes.
    I want to show him snowdrops   the gleam of them

spreading beneath the last crab apple tree
    where in soft evenings we bagged the falls

to make jelly. This was our walk   every day   around
    blazing hawthorns now broken bonfire sticks

stolen by storms. And here   what remains of a seat
    we called ours   worn pleachers

warm as setting sun   bones left to sink
    ghosts of blossomed boundaries

scent of honeysuckle   eglantine
    that clung to long summers   our summers

carried on air   sweet and heavy as the few steps
    he barely takes these days.

I scrape my boots at the door carrying our gift
    falling through my hands like rain.

PINE NEEDLES ON THE WINDOWSILL

When I can't sleep
I stand at my open window
and breathe in the truth of darkness.
I breathe the language of trees –
conversations we shared like drops of rain
between muddled branches empty of birds.
And out there in the slow night
I watch my children holding on
swinging above the river,
the hunger of deer in snow and old Ruby hen
who couldn't find her way home and froze.
I smell bonfire smoke – a year's brash
rising like a scarf through the giant pine, cones
falling hard to be gathered for winter – the long
goodbye, the missing, the mist between us
wrapping her cold arms around me
wanting to be my friend. Those everyday gifts
like the promise of snow
melting the moment they are offered.
I touch fifty springs, summers and autumns
all rolled into these tiny needles
I used to wipe away.

ACKNOWLEDGEMENTS

Roll Top - published in The Alchemy Spoon Issue 2 Metal 2020
From a Balcony - 3d Prize in The Pre-Raphaelite Society Competition 2021
Published in *A Passion* Hedgehog Press 2023
My Body is a House In Winter - published in Boats Against the Current 2022
Moss - 1st Prize in the Indigo Dreams Spring Prize. Published in Reach Poetry 2023
Love - Highly commended in IAmInPrint competition 2023
In the Garden Where We Sit Together published in Dust Magazine Issue 12 2024
Take Me With You - Longlisted in The Rialto Nature & Place competition 2024
For the Love of a Fellside - published by Ink Sweat & Tears 2025
Quilt - Longlisted in The Plough Prize & shortlisted in The Bridport Prize 2025
In the Wooden House - 2nd Prize in Canterbury Poet of the Year 2025
Heirlooms - shortlisted in Cheltenham Poetry Competition 2025
To Fill the Space - published in *To Lay Sun Into A Forest* anthology Sidhe Press 2025
Wallers - 3rd Prize in Indigo Dreams Spring Prize and published in *Reach* Poetry, Indigo Dreams 2025 and *Through-stone and Thread,* Wyvern Press 2026

Cover painting *Adoration* by Stephen Darbishire RBA

I'd like to thank all these publishers and competitions judges for awarding me with prizes and publishing my poems, especially during challenging times.
Huge thanks to all who have helped with some of these poems: Kathleen Jones. Ilse Pedler. Kelly Davis. Thanks to Ilse Pedler, Jane Burn and Kathleen Jones for their thoughtful and uplifting endorsements. To my husband Stephen for his constant support, our years together and for painting the cover image, *Adoration*. Huge thanks to Mark Davidson for having faith in this collection and for bringing it into the world.

Poetry is an essential focus and true healer.

ALSO BY KERRY DARBISHIRE

A Lift of Wings - Indigo Dreams 2014
Kay's Ark - Handstand Press 2016
Distance Sweet on my Tongue - Indigo Dreams 2018
Glory Days – a collaboration with Kelly Davis - Grey Hen Press 2021
A Window of Passing Light - Dempsey & Windle 2021
A Passion - Hedgehog Press 2022
Jardinière - Hedgehog Press 2022
River Talk - Hedgehog Press 2024. Winner of The Wordsworth Prize for Literature and Poetry, Lakeland Book Awards 2025

Signed books can be found on: www.darbishirearts.co.uk

Social Media:
Bluesky: @kerrydarbishire.bskysocial
X: @kerrydarbishire
Facebook: StephenKerryDarbishire

www.ingramcontent.com/pod-product-compliance
Lightning Source LLC
Chambersburg PA
CBHW021639080526
44584CB00015BA/1616